way to go

way

to go

poems

RICHARD SANGER

BIBLIOASIS / *windsor, ontario*

FIRST EDITION
10 9 8 7 6 5 4 3 2 1

Library and Archives Canada Cataloguing in Publication

Title: Way to go / Richard Sanger.
Names: Sanger, Richard, 1960-2022, author.
Description: Poems.
Identifiers: Canadiana (print) 20220465436 | Canadiana (ebook) 20220465479 | ISBN 9781771965538 (softcover) | ISBN 9781771965545 (EPUB)
Classification: LCC PS8587.A3723 W39 2023 | DDC C811/.54—dc23

Edited and designed by Vanessa Stauffer
Copyedited by Emily Donaldson

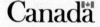 

Published with the generous assistance of the Canada Council for the Arts, which last year invested $153 million to bring the arts to Canadians throughout the country, and the financial support of the Government of Canada. Biblioasis also acknowledges the support of the Ontario Arts Council (OAC), an agency of the Government of Ontario, which last year funded 1,709 individual artists and 1,078 organizations in 204 communities across Ontario, for a total of $52.1 million, and the contribution of the Government of Ontario through the Ontario Book Publishing Tax Credit and Ontario Creates.

PRINTED AND BOUND IN CANADA

acknowledgements: *Arc, Canadian Notes and Queries,*
The Fiddlehead, Literary Review of Canada, Malahat Review,
The New Quarterly, Toronto Star, Vallum, The Walrus.

thanks: Naomi Campell, Christopher Clark, Geoffrey Cook,
Harold Hoefle, Deborah Lambie, Mark Migotti, Louis Sanger,
Malcolm Sanger, Carmine Starnino, Vanessa Stauffer,
Ricardo Sternberg, Dan Wells.

contents

i.

INTO THE PARK

Into the park in late summer on your bike,
the sudden chill of trees and shade, the breeze
down the front of your shirt
cool against your chest, linen rippling
a frisson tingling your nipples,
as the afternoon heat
lingering
on the grass starts to retreat,
the bike whirrs and into the park you go,
deeper, this is your park, you know
its groves, its benches, its three-storey trees,
depressions where rain gathers, puddles freeze,
and it changes every time—
that's why you come, the anticipation,
you don't know what you'll find here,
as the shadows grow in the bushes, or who
you'll meet at the bench
someone you know,
or someone new,
or someone you knew
a long time ago
now with eyes that have seen so much more
and lines in his face, or hers,
and deeper you go and further back
no idea what you'll say when you meet, or do,
what new arrangements or conspiracies you'll fall into,
what raw truths,
what entanglements, what dangers.

THE SANDS

Frown and wrinkled lip he's got. Sunk in himself
on the sidewalk, head the same height
as the briefcases and exhaust pipes,
he sneers at the coins that drop. Taxis idle,
then pull out, buff his face with fumes.
When he coughs, it's a truck that won't start
some subzero morning in the trailer park.
Once it was his foot on the pedal, the tunes
blasting as he tore up the highway
to Fort Mac, Fort Chip. But he can't go back,
not to that landscape. The tar, the trees, the sands,
the traplines that were his kingdom…All gone.
And the machines he drove—colossal wrecks—
rust like dinosaurs beside the tailing ponds.

WAS IT

Driving early one spring morning
out of the city, the two boys
in the back seat playing peek-a-boo,
the city, all glass, girders, concrete,
strip malls, Costcos, service stations
sprouted up here and there
so we can keep driving, taking the city
further and further out, and still find
not a speck of green in sight,
not a tree or leaf—is this what we do,
pave, encase, squish the living sap
out of the earth?—and now a laugh,
a titter starts and won't cease, was it for this,
a giggle, a chortle deep-throated
like a crack opening in the asphalt
or a brook in early spring
galloping down a wooded slope,
over stones, sticks and clumps of ice,
was it for this we made the roads,
rampaged ahead without a thought,
over every obstacle we found:
dead black leaves, tree bark, rocky outcrops,
for this, we dynamited granite,
cut through hillsides, flattened the planet,
pausing only to regroup, catch
ourselves, reflect in pools and eddies,
at traffic lights, and then erupt,
chuckling, roaring again? Was it?

HOP HORNBEAM

It's March, tender one, and still
you cling to your feelings,
these precious leaves of yours
you won't let go. Remember the fall
when the big trees unbuttoned,
unburdened themselves of all
that gaudy trash they dash off?
How it fluttered down and collected
in the ditches and gutters,
yellow and orange and hectic red?
You skulked in their shade,
tut-tutting at their profligate ways,
how they spend themselves
before it's even November,
as you wait, wait for the right breeze
to launch your little babies…
You'll be like Borges' scholar,
so enchanted by the magic
of words on a page, you end up
leading a life as thin and pale
as the paper between your fingers—
these whispers of worn parchment,
the leaves you can't bear to part with
that tug and tatter in the breeze.

PADDLE

The black cherry paddle my mum, long dead,
gave my father, recently arrived on these shores,
and hoped he'd use to steer his Canadian sons
through the choppy waters ahead—

oh I've sanded and revarnished its grain
to a lovely auburn shade—
red like my mother's hair was red, red like a flame
you can douse in water again and again.

I ask if he'd like to take it with him
when he sets out to join her on the other shore
in place of a heraldic device
or the kind of gift the pharaohs would adorn

their funerary boats with. "Oh no, you keep it.
I plan on swimming the Styx," the old soldier says,
—he did his National Service in Egypt—
"After all, I swam the canal at Suez."

CANOE

1.

Viewed from the side, the familiar curve
rises up to venture forth, buoyant,
full-breasted, womanly; glides above
those less-endowed, less in the current,
parting them, well, like a knife through butter.
Behind, her shy twin turns the other cheek,
metes out one single thread on the water
to stitch up the havoc her sister wreaks.
From above, her hips could bear whole families,
and their baggage into new worlds, waltz you
through the rockiest bed, the tightest channel.
So take her by the hips, get down on your knees
and feel how she sinks, sways and resists you
with every rib. Push off, wet your paddle.

2.

That's one way of putting it, I suppose—
the canoe as the chalice
of all the delusions we most cherish,
the shape we took from those
whose lands we stole to settle and hold in sway,
and which you, the most disreputable,
in the slimiest way imaginable,
now liken to a woman's curves…One way
you could but would best avoid putting it—
Would but won't, as is your wont. Oh, just run
your fingers down the grain of gunwale and rib,

would you, feel the pine, the cedar cede
to your purpose, the wood bend all in worship.
What other vessel could you love like this?

3.
Push off, wet
that paddle,
the wobble
correct
with a shift
of your rear
then steer
against the drift
of the current
the tip
as you point
the way through,
oh trip,
oh canoe.

MAY 1968

(In May 1968, journalist Blair Fraser drowns on the Petawawa River.)

Yes, Jeanie's in Paris. Just so's you know,
there are rapids up ahead... The Rollway.
We're portaging them. Take-out's on the right.
Hell, I'm not worried. Told her we're going down
the Petawawa, our kids are all away,
have yourself some fun. Just look at that cliff,
would you? Must be 100 metres high—
sheer, but with that hemlock sticking out,
like a dart flung, hanging on for dear life...
So she said Paris. No idea all hell
was about to break loose there...You heard?
Students in the streets, tear gas, barricades.
wouldn't surprise me if de Gaulle himself
turned tail and fled. I love France, love the French
but such a good life and they're never content.
She's got a friend there, married a local—
Things are a bit rocky. Some river, eh?
It's the most fun you can find in Algonquin.
Last year, just upriver, Trudeau dumped—
Good sport he was once we got him out,
jumped up and shook himself off like a puppy.
Would I mind? She got through before we left,
I could hear them chanting slogans down the line,
her voice bubbling over with excitement.
I'm having my adventure and she, hers—
if that includes a little tumble, so be it.
I mean, imagine going all that way,
and not? The water's so high you can't tell

where the rapids are. The take-out's coming up.
That damn Trudeau: one year you're soaking wet,
getting swarmed by blackflies in the backwoods;
the next, you're PM and the women are
lining up to toss their panties at you…
It's as if all the pressures, desires, urges
in the world rose to the surface, swirling, rose
and burst, they pick you up and sweep you off,
you can't control them, you just have to ride
the current as best you can—I saw him
at his rally in April, and caught this look
in his eyes, bemusement or pure terror,
I couldn't tell—things happen so fast,
you've no choice, no time to think, you're just
a plaything of fate, you try not to miss
what you—what's that?—set out for, not forget
what you wanted to achieve, and why,
your higher calling, newspapers, politics,
holy cow, we missed it, you end up, shit,
we're in it now, doing things you never thought,
clinging to any scrap, Christ, there's a rock,
trying desperately to stay on top,
some float—here goes—to high office, some don't.

GONE SOUTH

Nothing for him here, Teacher said, looking out
at the houses we got, busted screens, the forest.
He's bright, deserves the chance. Teach was right:
I had six of them, three left. Little Peter, the sharpest,
sparky-eyed, bushy-tailed, he'd climb up into my lap
to show me his things: the frogs he'd caught,
the sticks he'd carve. When I got the phone,
he taught me to use it, taught me Angry Birds.
He was going to build things, be an engineer
so we let him go. I was only South
the once when Jason was sick, I don't know
what stuff our kids get up to down there.
Sure, they change, but Teach said it would stop him
from mixing with the wrong crowd here.
When they called, the Radio Lady came out to ask
what it felt like, she wanted me to talk.
I tried to say things she wanted to hear
but I just had questions. He was high, they said,
and fell off a balcony…
Balcony? We got nothing like that up here.

FILM INTERRUPTED

So quickly it comes to an end, the film,
you can hardly remember the start—
a garden, lilacs, some comic fun and confusion
as the gorgeous young things depart

on love's merry song and dance...
There was a picnic, was there not?
A kiss, tearful reproaches, a lonely walk
down a cobbled street to the port,

a ravishing face that vanished
and one that doesn't. A tanker explodes.
Kids run in and out of a house.
A man is wrestling with the codes.

The doors spring open, downstairs: wine,
laughter, glowing faces and brows knitted
as a stranger expounds her grand theory
—you nodded off, admit it—

and now you awake in a cold white room,
neck and body aching, the same voice is
still talking but no one laughs any more.
Listen closer. It's your diagnosis.

NOVEMBER RUN
for Harold Hoefle

I read your letter, Harold,
as one nurse describes her new dessert
—rice krispie squares, peanut butter, chocolate—
to another who hooks me up to my IV drip
and I want nothing more than to go
for a run with you as wild
and muddy and unpredictable
as your letter, a long November run
to commemorate the races we never ran
against each other, the OFSAAs we never placed;
I want to head off hanging on your shoulder
—light-footed, loose-limbed, easy-breathing—
as you lead the way along the gravel shoulder
of the highway out of town, past the 7/11,
the gas station, the monster homes,
then cut off down a path into the woods
and up whatever kind of hills you have
in Sainte-Anne-de-Bellevue, or pastures
overgrown with sumac, I suppose,
or maybe we'd go for a run in the Gatineau,
why not, hell, up and down those ski trails,
over branches and rocks and puddles and streams
when there are still a few leaves
left on the hardwoods and also perhaps
a few precocious snowflakes in the air
appearing like over-keen students
to try their luck and melt on contact
as our cheeks and thighs redden,

and now you hang on my shoulder
as I lead the way, taking you on, pressing the pace
until we fall into a rhythm, brisk, mechanical,
each of our bodies telling the other's
I can do this all I want, I can cream you,
our bones and sinews making themselves known
shedding all superfluous weight and thought,
as we run those Gatineau trails and this steep slope
and I attack, putting my forehead into it,
pumping my arms, thinking now I can do it,
administer the *coup de grâce*,
and leave you in the dust…No such luck.
At the crest, you're still with me, surprise,
and so we head back, lungs panting, thighs aching,
letting our legs freewheel as fast as they can,
you ahead of me, or me ahead of you
breathing down my neck, laughing,
ready to pick me off and whoosh past
to the chalet where there'll be showers and beer,
some women who'll understand our jokes,
who'll ooh and ahh over our mud-spattered calves,
and tell us we're full of shit, if necessary,
and a roaring fire to get roaring drunk beside
as we proceed to purify the dialect of the tribe
and forge in the exuberance of our talk
the only lightly embellished story of our race.

WAYS TO GO
for Natalie

Up a slope in early spring, into a stand
of hardwoods, last fall's leaves now black
and spongy underfoot, the way ahead
not exactly dark or difficult, but gone.

    *

The doctor has spoken with you.
Can you explain, in your own words,
what you think your diagnosis is?

    *

Spores, fungi, mycelia, frilly bonnets,
tuberous new growths, elaborate arabesques
and turkey tails sprouting from old trunks...
The intestines of the forest digest
the news: what's outside also grows inside us.

    *

So haul out the artillery, hook me up
and chemo carpet-bomb the rebel zones
into submission... All set? Here we go.

RELEASE

In taking up this wayward string of words
(hereinafter "Poem"), in a manner
either deliberate or accidental,
paid for or freely happened upon,
the Reader (hereinafter "you")
assumes all risk of personal trauma,
loss, or misfortune resulting from the lines,
images, or infelicities of said Poem,
including, but not limited to, acts of God,
real or imagined, high winds, avalanches,
lightning strikes, floods, the tree branch that may,
without warning, crash down on the café
where you sit reading this one afternoon
as well as all acts of human thoughtlessness
and cruelty, such as hurtful words or slurs,
black eyes, broken hearts, torn or soiled garments
civil unrest, head-on collisions, war;
in addition, you as the Reader agree
to release the Poet (hereinafter "me")
from all liability, claim, or cost
for any damage sustained in situations
that can be reasonably derived from the Poem,
extremes of temperature and emotion,
surprising desires acted upon, or left to fester,
any such altercations or contagions
as may occur or be transmitted
between consenting adults of any age or gender,
all resulting states of rapture or paranoia,

all losses of property or innocence,
all forms of disillusionment, religious or sexual;
furthermore you hereby acknowledge that
as the free and independent interpreter
of these inky impressions (hereinafter "letters")
you bear full and complete responsibility
for all such calamities as they may describe,
and are, for all legal and moral purposes,
therefore also the Poet (hereinafter "you")
and author of your own misfortunes,
such as they may be mirrored in the Poem.

THE SKI-DOO

—Where, Sally, just where have you been?
It's already half past six
and we're invited out to dinner.
We're going to the Schmidts'.

—Sorry, Mum, I was at the bridge
the ice is breaking up.
—But I told you to come straight home
and now we'll have to rush.

—Have you seen how high the river is?
how dark and fast it runs?
It's like a gang of Hell's Angels
gunning their bikes through town.

—Now go upstairs and get ready,
find something nice to wear.
We're going to the Schmidts' for dinner
and Edward will be there.

—There were slabs of ice the size of trucks
and one we waited for
that hung there, massive, like a tanker
fastened to the shore.

— Mrs. Schmidt has been planning this
ever since it was Christmas.
Edward's home for his reading week.
He's at Queen's, doing Business.

—I know. She told us all about him.
—You'll want to look your best.
—We're late. Just let me go like this.
—Why not put on a dress?

—But there's no time. —That's your fault:
I told you to come quick.
—I was watching the ice break up
—I know who you were with.

—Tell me. —It's Danny Bradeski, of course!
—How do you know? —Who else?
That's why your bra-strap's twisted out
and your cheeks are flushed.

—You always think that! —I know you.
—You're wrong. It was a dare.
—Hurry up, Sally, or we'll be late
and Edward —I don't care!

It was a dare. Danny's friends bet him
he couldn't take his Ski-Doo
from Hunters' Bay to Fairy Lake.
He said that's what he'd do.

—What? They dared him to drive his Ski-Doo
  over that open stretch?
—Haven't you seen the boys do that?
—But it'll sink like lead.

—You start the Ski-Doo off on ice
  and hit the water fast.
  That's why we waited till the current
  had taken the last slab.

—He rode the river right through town
  while the whole town watched?
—Everyone was out on the bridge!
—Because of that show-off.

—The mayor, the priest, and the mechanic,
  they all snuck out to watch.
  I even saw our principal there
  pretending he was lost.

Miss Singh, the science teacher, came
  to film it on her phone.
  Mike Mackenzie, the hockey coach,
  was jumping up and down

—But you didn't see the Schmidts out there,
  they don't go in for such
—We stood there till Mike heard the roar
  and told us all to shush

Danny came swerving round the corner.
You should have seen him go!
Like a duck, the way it flies over
the water, fast and low,

His sled skimmed the surface and left
this roostertail behind
as long as he kept moving forward,
Miss Singh said he'd be fine.

We watched him come under the bridge,
banking round the S-bend
and vanish. He waved, the river roared,
it only took a second.

—And he made it? —You bet —Good lord,
I'll call and say we're late.
—Don't bother, Mum. —Just come like that.
—But I've decided … —What?

—I'm not going —But Edward's come.
He's good-looking and bright …
—Danny B. can sled on water
He's taking me tonight.

PAINTER, MUSE, MONEY

1.

He was hungry so he decided to paint a picture he could sell. He asked his lover to sit for him and, because she was hungry too, she agreed. He told her they would get more for the painting if she took her clothes off and so she did. In fact, he knew of a certain collector who would be particularly interested in such a picture. He had seen this collector looking closely at his lover with her clothes on.

2.

But wouldn't he be jealous? she asked. The rich, they can buy everything! Oh, but it wouldn't really be her, he said. It would just be a painting, a fake. He would take care of that. He would still have her and she would still have him. With her he could make all the paintings he ever wanted and they would never really be her. And they both would have money, for a change.

3.

So he made the painting and sold it. He liked having money. So did she. So he made more paintings of her naked in different poses which he sold to other collectors who had seen the first painting. With the money he made, he bought food, wine, things—and he paid her. What did she buy with the money she got? Clothes.

4.

Clothes, extravagant clothes, she bought to wear out, to wear to parties. Silk scarves, a kimono, an ostrich-feather hat…They were artists, weren't they? One day, the painter decided that he wanted to paint her in the hat but that the hat she had was the wrong colour. He went out and bought her a new lime-green ostrich-feather hat. Chartreuse, in fact. He painted her in the hat. She liked the painting a lot and so did his dealer, who hung it in the window of his gallery, where other people could see it. The painter was right: lime-green was the best colour for the hat. She started to wear the hat when she went out to parties so people would know it was her, the woman in the lime-green ostrich-feather hat.

5.
They got invited to more and more parties, and met more and more people…After a few years, they split up. The usual: he wanted to paint someone new, someone younger. And she went with another man, older, who had more money and paintings.

6.
Actually it happened like this. The art collector saw her across the room and came up to her. He knew her face. Where had he seen her before? Oh, that's where. But now he was meeting the original. Was he disappointed? Oh, no, it was a pleasure.

7.
One day he took her to his country house, where he kept his paintings. This was long after they had first got together and slept together. In fact, she was getting tired of him and he was looking for new things to do. He wanted to keep her. He said he had something to show her, to give her.

8.

So she found herself standing in front of the first painting her lover had made of her all those years ago, long before all the posh parties and the ostrich-feather hat. It wasn't her. She didn't have that dark beauty mark on the side of her left breast, did she? It wasn't her—that uncharacteristic tentative pose, those lithe limbs, those eyes that only wanted to please, that beseeched. Not her, this young waif so obviously out of her element, this lean animal whose tensed fingers betrayed her desperation, her striving. No, she, the lover, had poise, social ease and grace, unlike this model. The collector looked on, with eyes of his own that only wanted to please. It wasn't her but now it was hers.

BRORA

(i.m. John Lambie)

If we're not at the station, wait at the wee café on the platform
    (they have tea and the biscuits your mother likes);
if the mannie's not there and the caff's closed, there's the
    newsagents; they won't mind you in there to keep out of
    the weather;
if, after a decent interval, we haven't appeared, I'd say the Royal
    Marine;
if you stay in the bar, it's really quite reasonable for a hotel;
if you don't feel smart enough, try the Sutherland Arms instead;
    some English folk have bought it; white settlers, we call
    them; they're not too posh;
if you're in a real fix, the Braes, though I haven't darkened those
    doors for years;
if they hadn't closed the coal mine, it would never have got like
    that with Ewan and his mates in there from noon to night;
if you think of it, all dark and dreich, it's no different from being
    down a mine;
if you go up to the new Tourist Bureau they built where the pit
    was, you'll see how the coal shafts went way out beneath
    the sea for miles and miles; aye, they did;
if we don't find you in the Braes, it may be that the burn's over-
    run its banks and we've
been caught up at the loch;
(if you remember, that's where your mother took me cycling
    when I first came up to work at the wireless station);
if that's not it, we may be out for a wee gander on the Back Shore
    and have simply lost track of time;

if they hadn't closed the wireless, you might see young Dougie
    just getting off his shift, coming out the gate where your
    mother used to meet me;

if he hasn't intercepted some signals from the Russians, and had
    to tell GCHQ Cheltenham;

if the tide's out, there's all manner of winkles and shells and
    treasure to find along with the usual seals;

if the sandpipers and curlews have been around, there'll be lots
    of Russian signals and Cyrillics to study in the wet sand;

if we're lucky, we might see a school of dolphins leaping (Angus
    from the garage saw them last week);

if not, there are the oil-rigs off in the North Sea to look at;

if we haven't gone out for a walk, it may be my chest; just a bit
    funny these days; not my usual;

if we have, you'd best make your own way home, you remember
    the way;

if they hadn't closed the wool mill, you'd still hear the horn at
    quarter to eight in the mornings, the way you did when you
    were a girl;

if they hadn't invented this polar fleece business;

if you come along the river, there may be a few men in the gorse
    bushes, fishing; young Charlie's lot have taken to poaching;

if you see one pull in a salmon, just pretend you've seen nothing;
    lots of unemployed in the village these days; chômeurs, you
    call them in French;

if you come the other way, don't be surprised;

if your bag's heavy, you may want to rest a moment and look up
    at the burns and braes;

if it's the right time of day, you'll see the sunlight in the heather

if I'm feeling better, I may come down the road to meet you;

if they hadn't closed the coal mine
if we're not on the platform and we're not at the hotels
if I'm not feeling better
if they hadn't closed the wireless
if you can decipher the sandpiper's Cyrillics
if we haven't gone out for a walk
if you make your own way home
if you come in the back door, you may not see me
if I'm sitting in the front room,
if they hadn't closed the wool mill
if you remember the way
if you come in and I'm in my chair
if I look older and frailer
if I'm asleep, I may not hear you
if you rub my feet
if you don't mind
if I wake up and smile
if I say your name
if you're not shocked at how I've changed
if you find your way
if it's still home
if the town's still here
if I'm here
if I'm still I
if not
if I'm still
if I'm gone
if I'm
if

VARIATIONS
(For Rebecca Campbell)

If someone had told me, I'd probably have then and there.

If someone had told me I'd be then and there, I'd probably have.
But.

If someone had told me "slit my wrists," I'd probably have then
and there. But I'd be.

If someone had told me but I'd slit my wrists, I'd probably be
singing then and there.

If someone had told me thirty years ago I'd be singing "slit my
wrists" at Grossman's, I'd probably have then and there. But.

If someone had slit their wrists at Grossman's, I'd probably have
told them but on Friday afternoons I'd be singing covers.
Then and there thirty years ago.

If someone had told me thirty years ago I'd be singing covers at
Grossman's on Friday afternoons, I'd probably have slit my
wrists then and there. But now that I'm here, it's kind of
wonderful.

SPANISH SONGS

1. Violeta Parra, "Gracias a la vida"

> *Alone and in a very low voice, dripping with sarcasm, a little man,*
> *one of those tiny dancers that suddenly appear from out of the*
> *brandy bottles, said "¡Viva Paris!" as if saying "Here we don't care*
> *about your abilities, your technique or your fame. Here we care*
> *about something else."*—Lorca

Sunday mornings at the Marché aux Puces,
you'd hail a survivor of the night before
with "Comrade," huddle round your coffee for warmth,
dissecting the paper and Reagan's latest ruse
—or Borges'—as the Chilean exiles stood
and hawked alpaca sweaters in the rain.
A Vespa brought reinforcements. The topic changed.
You left to look for poems, as best you could,
amongst the junk, then rendezvous for couscous
and, later still, in the foreign students' dorm,
start a new movement with Pilar, or Luz
—identical rooms, ephemeral joys—
until one night, in one of those rooms,
echoing, unforgettable, that voice:

I thank life
for all it has given me.
For the two eyes in my head
which allow me to tell
black from white, green from red,

42

to see the constellations
in the heavens above
and in the city crowds
the man whose face I love.

I thank life
for all it has given me.
It's given me tears
and it's given me laughter.
This way I can tell
what joy is, and disaster.
This way the words I sing
for you, and the chords
I play, aren't mine alone—
this way my song is yours.

2. Estrella Morente, "Zambra"

Lo que en otros no envidiaban,
ya lo envidiaban en mí—Lorca

Estrella de la Aurora Morente Carbonell,
who the hell do you think you are,
dressing up like the Queen of Egypt
and singing about your broken heart?

—Get away from my window,
I'm about to sigh.
When I sigh, it's flames that come out
and they'll set you on fire.

Estrella Morente, I knew your father:
he was an artist and a gypsy through and through—
a voice like his had been to the wars.
He could sing about suffering, but you?

—My mother has a copper pot
she fills with her sorrows each night;
in the morning, she gives it a shake
and out jump little grains of rice.

Estrella Morente, your mother danced in the caves
and your husband, they say, 's killed five bulls;
come back and sing for us when some real tears
have etched their lines in those cheeks of yours.

—*What more can I give you,*
oh tell me what more.
Even the water I drink
I have to beg you for.

3. Concha Buika, "Volver, Volver"

La pura voz humana, empobrecida por el amor—Lorca

This love I can't leave behind, the voice sings,
as out from the wings
slips this teeny slip of life
has got me so worked up,
has dragged me round and tortured me so much,
I'm dying to go back, back to your arms again.
I don't care how much it hurts my pride,
how bad it looks, I'll do what it takes,
I'll crawl on my hands and knees,
I'll pull out my hair, I'll howl, I'll bleed…
I know how to love and how to lose,
I know exactly what it means, she sings
and holds the note—*volver, volver*—
surveying us, teary-eyed, utterly transported
in our upholstered seats,
takes one barefoot step back and breaks out laughing
in a great, gap-toothed Guinean grin:
Love, Love, Love! What a joke!
What am I doing here, singing to you
about that dirty old trick, of all things,
making you believe I know how it really feels
and yet would—she picks up the note—*go back,* she sings?

iii.

FLÂNEUR

Symptom Hall, the Purple Institution,
Muhtadi's, the Greeks, the Riv, the Bamboo,
the Elmo, the Ep, the Dip, the Cameron
(of course), the Horseshoe and the Last Temptation,
the Lounges, Lula, Lava and I.V,
and the Rooms, Red, Green, Orbit and Hugh's,
Baby Huey, Opera Bob's and Ted's Collision,
Sneaky Dee's and Sweaty Betty's
Clinton's, the Imperial, the Victory,
the Done Right Inn and By The Way
the basement Goran kept on Carlton
one summer I was short on friends and luck…
I drank in all of you—I drink you all in,
your suds, your solace; I haven't had enough.

ODE TO CLAUDE

A blustery fall day, University Ave,
just north of Queen's Park and just across from
the Royal Ontario Museum,
a trenchcoat bustles past, and I stop,
turn, look back ... Then the penny drops:
Claude Bennett! The snappy business-like walk,
the smartly-parted hair and squeaky-clean cheeks,
the lethal teeth, the navy-blue suits
and those eyes that seemed almost to simulate thought ...
Claude Bennett, the very symbol
and truest emblem of my youth!
You were a provincial politician
with the stress on provincial.
Every election, your blue-rinsed troops would rout
through all the church basements
and Legion Halls of Ottawa South.
And every morning you swam your half-miles—
strange how, from the piles and piles
of glossy brochures that were your campaigns,
the one thing my mind retains
is the picture of you in a powder-blue pool,
gingerly clutching the edge, with your glasses on.
For Ontario, like you, like your pool,
was Tory blue in those days,
the tulips alone along the Driveway were red,
and I, I was growing up.
Through high school, bicycles and hockey sticks.

Through razors, band-aids and the hit-parade of CFRA.
And you, I like to think,
were there every step of the way:
the treks we made across the bridge
to buy beer in Quebec, at the friendly epicerie,
I remember you walking beside us
as we hauled the cases home over the icy slush,
like Scott's expedition to the South Pole,
half-frozen, half-delirious,
all of thirteen, and getting pissed.
Then the night Willy MacPherson
blew his first UIC cheque
on some white powder we called "mesc"
and took turns ingesting while, outside,
as if by magic, the year's first snow
promptly fell? I saw you there, Claude Bennett,
sticking out like a sore thumb
or a secret policeman in the Daveys' kitchen,
and then rolling around outside in white stuff,
completely out of control. Yes, it was fun.
And, best of all, the night you missed,
the night Annie Davey and I
jumped in the Rideau Canal for a midnight dip,
our white skin glistening. We swam a bit,
laughed and splashed and had just begun to kiss
when two cops shouted with a megaphone:
SWIMMING IN THE CANAL IS PROHIBITED.
Claude, if we'd invited you along,
I'm sure you would have pulled us out.
The water, though, was welcoming and warm

and filthy, of course, and I liked it, I did:
the water that collected everything,
our laughs and splashes, our little gasps,
the movements of light rippling on the surface
and each hidden, uninhibited limb,
such highs and lows, the scarves and mitts
we lost skating in long-since melted drifts,
the popsicle wrappers dropped, the pay-offs you got,
the slush funds, the trust funds, the husbands,
the kisses, the condoms, the tears of the teenage mums,
all the things you pretended didn't exist,
at least not in Ottawa South, all drifting off,
drifting under the Bank Street Bridge;
nights that were fun, nights that weren't,
nights we didn't know which was which,
we just hung around, the girls we hung around with,
Jane, Kate and Annie, lovely red-headed Annie,
and all the other nights and girls that have gone,
gone for good. What happened, Claude, what happened?
For all any of us cared,
you might as well have been a mannequin
modelling spotless high-rise underwear
in the Eaton's catalogue. Yes, I know
you were a cabinet minister once
but that was in another province
and, besides, it was long, long ago.
Tell me instead what you dreamt of,
what new waters, what pools, who you phoned
when you got the bends, tell me if love
played any role or led you around ... No, don't.

Pull yourself together, dry that eye,
extend your hand, say Hi-how-ya-doing-Fine,
smile and walk on. Just like old times.
That's it. Do as I say now, Claude. Goodbye.

NATIONAL ORGANS

1. *The Globe and Mail*

The subject who is truly loyal—
and none more loyal than you, dear Mum,
to our national organ, *The Globe and Mail*,
how you would count on it plus a mug
of black coffee to kickstart your day,
to remind you of all you were against,
the appointed faces of the ROB
blithely smiling, those eminently
dim suits you schooled and squashed with,
and the things you were for, the camaraderie
of the letters page, Eugene Forsey
setting straight some sloppy story
with a caustic aside, what pleasure,
the editors' heads rolling, and the years—
Those arbitrary measures to which
We must all advise and submit.

2. *Sunday Morning*

Sunday morning and the usual Brit,
some itinerant mid-list book-tour toff, 'll
mistake your show for the pulpit
on which to bang on about her awful
childhood, or husband, or his latest stroll
through the slums of Chittagong
or Bloomsbury's dirty undies, each vowel
stretching out so fabulously long
it could swallow Saskatchewan,
she, or he, just loving the sound of him,
or her, imparting these pearls to us,
the great unwashed, until it's just too, too much:
with wit, with gravitas, like a knight
girding his steed, you interject
one deft "But surely" and the guest
is lanced. Thank you, Michael Enright.

THE NAMES THAT KICK

When I grow up, I want to play for Holland.
I'll wear bright orange,
my hair a shock of bottle blond
or seaweed-dark and tangled;
skin as brown as Sumatran cigarillos
or pale as Gouda cheese...
Yes, yes, I'll wear all these
and a name that really kicks—
like Jaap Stam, Wilfred Bouma, or Edgar Davids.

When I grow up I want to play for Holland.
I'll wear bright orange
and take the ball and
go weaving through the English midfield
with a shake and a shimmy, a little flick-flack,
a pass off to Dirk Kuyt and a pass back
as I guide toward the den of St. George
the cross I'll hit with a delicate whack
and a name that really scores—
like Denny Landzaat, or Giovanni van Bronckhorst.

When I grow up I want to play for Holland.
I'll wear bright orange
and take the ball and take them all
through to face the Brazilians
and win the game we've never won
with a tip of my head and a tap of my toe
and a name of pure Netherlandish brilliance

that rasps the throat and roils the tongue,
that outyodels Ronaldinho,
a name that dips and thongs and booms and sings—
like Ruud van Nistelrooy, Phillip Cocu
or Jan Vennegoor of Hesselink!

LAST CHOSEN

The truth, raw and sudden: off to play soccer
with my sons, both now taller and faster than me,
young animals ready to fend for themselves
in the wild give-and-take of these pick-up games
we find in the park, there's the usual warm-up,
showing off, dribbling tricks, and shooting the shit
with the big shots till it's time to make teams,
the chosen captains taking turns choosing:
… and-and-and the primal schoolyard scene
comes back, recess at your new school, just arrived
with your strange diction and clothes,
the teams growing as the captains size you up,
each summoning the next player with a nod
or a grunt, some new nickname
that may stick for good. *Twinkle-toes,*
or *Beckham*, and you stare, silently imploring,
still waiting, still unchosen, and found wanting…
It's just a moment before the game begins
but already you see the rusted-out old beater
on the used-car lot, the wheezing bag of bones
dispatched on the shrinking ice-floe—
this is how it starts, and how it ends.

iv.

LET'S STAY IN
(after Baudelaire)

Be still, my sadness, and let me feel your brow.
You wanted evening to come. Look, it's here,
swallowing up the parks and streets, and how—
bringing cover to some; to others, fear.
Let them, reckless and young, like brief insects
swarm and dance and carouse their cares away,
chasing new thrills, new mates, catching their deaths.
Give me your hand, washed or not, come this way,
far from them, my sadness. We've had our day.
Now like high clouds turning, in the last sun,
pink, purple, scarlet, we'll glow and give way
with only each other left to impress
and the sheets, as we lie down and listen,
love, to night, like a long shroud, come for us.

that they *are nothing but a* bundle *or collection of*
different perceptions, *which succeed each other with*
inconceivable rapidity, and are in a perpetual flux and
movement... —Hume

You're saying the man I loved's just a part
you played, a story you made up. You're not
Paul Lefebvre? —I was him. —Not any more?
—I loved being him. I loved being with you.
—I never lied to you, I told you my name,
I told you the truth. —The truth! You want me
to tell you that? Can't you see it's just a story,
another alias to which you'll attach
all these feelings and ideas you invent?
We all pretend. —So I can't know your name?
—You know that you don't know. —Thanks, Plato.
Now you're going to claim the woman you love
is also just a part I play, a story
I make up...—We all pretend, we all change.
We're just bundles of sensation that succeed
each other with inconceivable speed.
One minute you're happy; the next you're enraged.
—I know who I am and where I come from
and I told you —You told me what suited you
in that particular moment —It was the truth.
—And I told you the same —You told me lies!
—Together we invented a story
that made us both feel new, rejuvenated,
one we both wanted to believe —And that's love?

—What else is it? —So: just a pack of lies,
a changeable fiction in which we find
new and flattering versions of ourselves,
shorn of all inconvenient facts, the past?
—Exactly: a pact between two happy dupes,
a willing suspension of disbelief.

VALENTINE

So our punk Juliet from down the street
has gone and washed her clothes—
I watch her string out t-shirts, panties, jeans,
torn, skimpy things, and, last of all, a sheet
against the twilit city sky.
I watch her, and I think of you
in a laundromat, in wet Scotland,
reading a Spanish play I would also read
as the first sheet we tumbled on
spun round and round; you, twenty-one,
all legs and vocab lists and woolly jumpers,
scribbling in the margins of your book
as the strangers came and went:
what were you thinking then,
were you erasing or underlining this guy
you'd let into your life? The machine stops.
You check inside; heads turn; no, it's not dry.
You add another 50p. I think of all the sheets we've shared,
sheets we've slept and sweated and wept on since,
sheets left in hotels, sheets washed, hung and dried
over and over, and in the mornings,
sheets of newspaper we've read,
and new snow outside scribbled with stories
of birdseed and squirrels, the sheets of our bed
creased and rumpled, and the life we've spilled.

The things I've tried to put down on paper,
sheets and sheets, never enough, never dry,

and then, in spring, the rain,
coming down in sheets...
I think of them, and this sheet I spread
for us to start again, anew,
our story in the dumbstruck dark,
two stick figures, a blank slate, me, you...
The lines on this sheet, the sheet I hang on this line:
it's dry, it's wet, it's yours, my Valentine.

MARCELO'S REPLY
(Response to Antonio Cicero's "Palavras aladas")

Trust a poet! Antonio, you write a poem
just to say you didn't really mean the words
you said when we made love. Thanks. Thanks a lot.
They were just "winged words" you let slip, speech acts
spurred by the moment, intended to achieve
a specific end—delicious, yes, but brief,
too brief—before you went back to your scribbling…
And you think I couldn't figure this out
after all those siestas I've spent with you
on your old futon in the Rua da Lapa
and then watching you grow antsy? *Post coitum,*
omne animal triste est. That's Latin.
But here's my question: How can I even know
you really mean the words you write now?

The written word, you know, is meant to last
and when you recall in print the things we said
—passionate, silly, untrue, vanished words—
it seems to me that you, like all your ilk,
are still pining for permanence, and most
of all when you try to convert those words
into so-called acts of the tongue—your phrase—
and other linguistic feats of the sort
I blush to name—which, you want to tell me,
will continue to enrapture us in future nights?
In future nights? This is what you got up
in a rush from the futon to write down?
This, your white-hot flash of inspiration…?
What you left me for? Well, scribble on. I'm gone.

THE WHIP-POOR-WILL
(Let Go of the Day Remixed)

for Chandler and Natalie

Let go of the day, he tells her
and come sit in the garden.
In the hall, their son Aaron plays piano.
Let go of the day, he says.
He's a poet-mathematician and knows
their numbers will soon add up.
Let go of the day, he urges her,
on her ninety-first birthday
but she's still making history, or remaking it.
There's always a paragraph to finish,
an impostor, a monument to interrogate;
a ville lumière, a Budapest, a portico,
a saxophone, Aaron starts to riff…
(He can play a thousand different things.)
It's the time of the whip-poor-will,
he says in the hall where Aaron plays
with his band—woodwinds, guitar, drums—
and friends sing the songs they love to play.
They're having so much fun, riffing on
all those crazy, jazzy, made-up sounds
—verandah, portico, vestibule, balustrade—
that make us laugh and smile and think:
When did we last hear the whip-poor-will?
Fractals make more fractals, poems more poems,
and some birds have only one song.
Come sit in the garden, he asks,
stay here with me while it darkens.

In the hall, their son plays, his friend sings
and, looking straight at us, thinks
now I am going to have to make you cry.
Some birds have only one song.
Let go of the day, let go of the day,
and the whip-poor-will's song is done.

DET UBEVISSTE SJELELIV

And what might that be, Mr. Coles?
Last night with *Little Bird*
up to quarter to three—
tracing the twists and turns
of the path your syntax,
sinuous, exhilarating, takes
through the forest of your heart,
chasing subject and verb,
negotiating the abrupt shifts
of register as you, like a monk
or courtier in some grand chateau
candlestick in hand
lead me down rear staircases
and roundabout passageways
ever deeper into the workings
of that great pile, always knowing,
so it seems, where you're going,
how to get to the great hall
where the noisy banquet might await us,
but, no, preferring this other route,
less-travelled, until we pull up short
in front of a locked door
on a landing where I turn
and through a small window see,
don't I, this pale face the moon showed
like a hand mirror in the night sky
floating—what your man called
the unknown life of the soul?

TOAST

So many springs and falls and pounces,
so many vintages crushed
and dripping through our fingers,
so many nights and letters ending love,
you'd think we'd long since drained the cup.
But from dark sources the wells replenish,
and, in the vase, two tulips clink their glasses.

THE OLDS, THE NEWS

Old folks, propped up, watching the news,
and it doesn't get any newer, does it,
the usual head administering the same steady drip
of outrages to worry about, the images
spilling catastrophically across the screen,
bombs, borders, airports, oil tankers,
London, Jakarta, Lagos, a frantic parade that stops,
returns us to the head, still perfectly coiffed.

… And on the sofa, this other head, nodding off,
eyes closed, mouth agape, sojourning
in some happier realm, briefly dead.
She stirs herself to life, to pick up the thread
of this plotless mess, as if taking on
the weight of the planet's latest sorrow
might somehow anchor here a moment more
a spirit restless, hankering to depart.

EXIT INTERVIEW

Animula, vagula, blandula—Hadrian

Have you done what you came here to do?
And when you were done, or not,
did you sit in some favourite spot
while the light streamed in
and do nothing for an afternoon, or two?
Did you ever drop
everything one morning to head off
and start something new?

Have you done what you came here to do?
Have you gone where you wanted to go?
Seen the rainforests of·Haida Gwaii
and their trees, swum the oceans,
left your footprints on sand and the snow
of mountain passes? And the great cities, too—
have you walked their boulevards and alleys,
watched the kids, say, of Istanbul at play
and heard their mothers calling?
And on your way home, did you ever stray
down the street after yours to see the houses,
the strange faces, and have them look at you?

Have you done what you came to do?
Have you sat and talked and laughed
with all the people you wanted to?
Seen the friends you swore you'd see once more?
And the dark-haired girl who'd smile, lopsided,

as you entered your usual café,
did you ever think of something to say
to her? To amuse and waylay her?
Did you love many people? In different ways
or the same one thing in each
lovely creature you pursued?
Did you love one person as long and as much
as you could till you stopped? Did you stop?
And then, one evening, start again? Or not?

Have you done what you came here to do?
And sadness, too, have you known it?
Did some sudden news, an accident,
cataclysm or banishment cut your life in two?
And leave you picking up the pieces?
Did you choose one path, alone and true,
and follow it through to its conclusion?
Did the great currents, the theories
and inventions, the upheavals and epidemics,
touch you? Did they buffet and blow you off course?
Make you change plans, directions, shoes?
Or barely quicken your pulse
while you nodded before the evening news?

Have you done what you came here to do?

THE AZORES

Plan, pack, look up the maps that show
all the places you meant to go,
—Santiago, Haida Gwaii, St. Petersburg—
all places you won't get to now
—Anatolia, Buenos Aires, Fontainebleau—
and the Azores where you went to go,
yes but no, you can't say that, so you didn't
make the hike round the dark headland
to see the bright trawlers in the harbour,
never felt the crunch of wildflowers
and hardened lava beneath your boots,
nor tasted the fish stew you won't wash down
with the famous, tarry wine of Pico
the tavernkeeper keeps pouring for you—
Obrigado, you went to go, to say no
but you don't need to now, have some more,
drink all the wine you want, savour
the crushed lavender, the sea, the lava,
because you don't have to hike home,
don't have to go to all the places
—Santiago de Cuba, Compostela, Manaus—
you meant to, went to go, wanted to, won't.

RITA LEISTNER

RICHARD SANGER (1960–2022) grew up in Ottawa and lived in Toronto. He published three poetry collections and a chapbook, *Fathers at Hockey* (2020); *Dark Woods* was named one of the top ten poetry books of 2018 by the *New York Times*. His plays include *Not Spain*, *Two Words for Snow*, *Hannah's Turn*, and *Dive* as well as translations of Calderon, Lorca, and Lope de Vega. He also published essays, reviews, and poetry translations.